XTREME JOBS

RODEO CLOWN

BY JOHN HAMILTON

A&D Xtreme
An imprint of Abdo Publishing | www.abdopublishing.com

Visit us at
www.abdopublishing.com

Published by Abdo Publishing Company, a division of ABDO, PO Box 398166, Minneapolis, Minnesota 55439. Copyright ©2016 by Abdo Consulting Group, Inc. International copyrights reserved in all countries. No part of this book may be reproduced in any form without written permission from the publisher. A&D Xtreme™ is a trademark and logo of Abdo Publishing Company.

Printed in the United States of America, North Mankato, Minnesota.
052015
092015

Editor: Sue Hamilton
Graphic Design: John Hamilton
Cover Design: Sue Hamilton
Cover Photo: AP
Interior Photos: John Hamilton-pgs 1, 2-3, 6 (top), 7 (top & bottom), 9 (top), 10, 11, 14, 15 (top & bottom), 16-17, 18, 19, 20-21, 27, 28, 29 (top & bottom), 30-31, 32; Robert Botts-pgs 4-5, 6 (bottom), 8, 9 (bottom left & right), 12, 13 (and inset), 24-25, 25 (inset), 26; Corbis-pgs 22-23.

Websites
To learn more about Xtreme Jobs, visit booklinks.abdopublishing.com. These links are routinely monitored and updated to provide the most current information available.

Library of Congress Control Number: 2015930948

Cataloging-in-Publication Data

Hamilton, John.
 Rodeo Clowns / John Hamilton.
  p. cm. – (Xtreme jobs)
ISBN 978-1-62403-758-0
1. Rodeo clowns–Juvenile literature. I. Title.
791.8--dc23
                    2015930948

CONTENTS

Rodeo Clowns

When rodeo clowns first enter the arena, they appear to be like any other kind of clown. They wear colorful costumes and have an arsenal of jokes. But behind the face paint, baggy pants, and colorful suspenders, these goofy entertainers have a deadly serious job—protecting fallen cowboys from angry bulls.

Oklahoma bullfighter Paul Bonds rescues a fallen cowboy. The rider walked away from this encounter with barely a scratch.

Two Kinds of Rodeo Clowns

The job of rodeo clown today is divided into two specialties. Traditional rodeo clowns entertain crowds between events with humorous sketches or by telling jokes. The other kind of rodeo clowns are called bullfighters. They are the unsung heroes of the rodeo. Their job is to protect cowboys when the bull rides are over. They do this by distracting the bulls. This gives cowboys enough time to safely escape the arena.

ENTERTAINERS

Traditional rodeo clowns are entertainers. They wear face paint and colorful baggy clothes. While the rodeo competition is taking place, they walk along the fence and talk to the audience. They call it "walk and talk." It's like standup comedy mixed with sports announcing.

Between rodeo events, animals are herded into the chutes and cowboys prepare for competition. Rodeo clowns fill the "down time" with comedy and entertainment. They keep the crowd excited.

Tim "Wild Thang" Lepard and his Team Ghost Riders.

COMEDY ACTS

Comedy acts are brief sketches that keep the crowd entertained while waiting for the next rodeo competition. Rodeo clowns love performing. They especially like making people laugh. In their acts, they use funny characters, or props such as carts that resemble miniature ambulances. Many clowns don't get paid much, but they love what they do.

Denny Halstead, four-time Canadian Pro-Rodeo Entertainer of the Year.

XTREME FACT – Many rodeo clowns have colorful nicknames, such as Crash, Hollywood, and Gizmo.

11

BARREL MEN

The traditional rodeo clown's job isn't all fun and games. Many double as "barrel men." They can be lifesavers during bull riding competitions. If a bucked-off cowboy gets into trouble, he runs behind the rodeo clown's large barrel, which is made of aluminum or steel. The barrels are padded inside and out, and can weigh as much as 150 pounds (68 kg).

The barrel man helps distract the bull until it is herded back to its pen. Sometimes the bull goes after the clown, forcing him to hide inside the barrel for protection.

XTREME FACT – Barrels are sometimes called "bomb shelters" or "clown lounges."

BULLFIGHTERS

Bullfighters are a special kind of rodeo clown. They are not like the matadors of Europe or Mexico, who fight with capes and swords. Rodeo bullfighters do not kill bulls. The bulls of North American rodeos are valuable animals. Rodeo bullfighters match wits with these one-ton (907-kg) beasts, distracting them so that cowboys can scramble to safety when their rides are over.

XTREME FACT – A group of bullfighters is sometimes referred to as "the cowboy protection team."

Bullfighters are trained professionals who put their lives on the line. Instead of entertaining the crowd, their main job is to distract a bull after it has bucked off a rider. This gives the cowboy precious moments to escape from the arena. Bullfighters have great timing, and are experts at predicting bull behavior.

TEAMWORK

Bullfighters usually work in teams of two or three. They will do almost anything to rescue cowboys who are in trouble. They will even throw themselves in front of rampaging bulls to distract them. Sometimes the safest place is right by the bull's side, in its blind spot. The bull can't charge while it twists around, trying to find the rodeo clown. Being a bullfighter takes nerves of steel and a deep understanding of animal behavior. Injuries are a common job hazard.

Bullfighter Will O'Connell leaps over a charging bull to rescue a fallen cowboy.

Sometimes cowboys get their hand stuck in the bull rope and get tossed around like a rag doll. They can also get thrown and trapped under a bull's feet. While one bullfighter distracts the bull, his teammate works to untangle the rider or guide him to safety.

Bullfighters can distract bulls by shouting at them, waving their arms, or tossing their hats in the air. Sometimes bullfighters even have to grab an angry bull by the horns!

XTREME FACT – Cowboys who get their hand stuck in the bull rope are said to be "hung up."

HISTORY

Rodeos began in the American West in the early 1800s. According to the Cowboy Hall of Fame, the very first organized rodeo started in 1869 in Deer Trail, Colorado. As rodeos became more popular, clowns were hired to entertain the crowds between events.

By the 1920s, aggressive Brahma bulls were introduced. They were exciting to ride but very dangerous. It became important for clowns to distract the bulls in order to protect fallen cowboys. Clowns started using barrels for protection by the 1930s. In time, specialized "cowboy protection teams" branched off from clown work. They are called "bullfighters" in today's rodeos.

In this 1937 photo from a rodeo in Sun Valley, Idaho, famous rodeo clown Jazbo Fulkerson uses an ingenious device to experience the thrill of bull riding without all the risks.

BULLFIGHTER TRAINING

As modern rodeos and rodeo clowns have become more professional, many schools have opened to teach beginners. It takes a long time to become an expert bullfighter. One needs quick reflexes, stamina, and a knowledge of animal behavior. After bullfighting school, beginners start by working in small rodeos. As they gain experience, they move up to bigger and better-paying jobs.

Many rodeo clowns do not go to special schools. They learn by experience. Some are former bull riders. Others learn how to handle bulls by living or working on farms and ranches.

A student bullfighter faces off against a bull.

PROTECTIVE EQUIPMENT

Bullfighters often wear the same kind of baggy clothes that traditional rodeo clowns wear. The brightly colored clothes and handkerchiefs flap around as the bullfighter runs, which helps distract the bulls. The baggy clothes are also designed to tear away if the bull's horns get snagged on them.

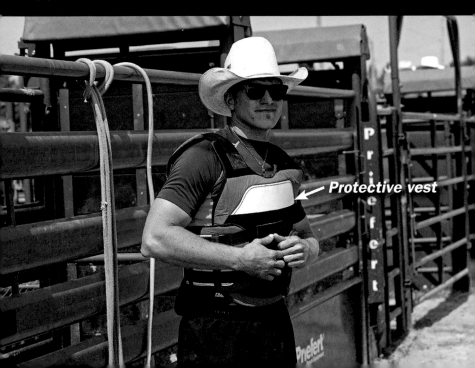

← *Protective vest*

Knee brace →

Hidden by their clothing, bullfighters wear protective vests. These hard plastic shells are often made of Kevlar and protect against crushing injuries. Bullfighters also usually wear knee and elbow pads. Some wear braces on joints that have been previously injured.

JOB FACTS

odeo clown salaries vary widely. Some may earn as much as $2,000 per rodeo. Others make much less, especially if the rodeo is small. Most rodeo clowns are male. Experienced rodeo clowns with busy schedules can earn more than $100,000 per year. However, they face on-the-job hazards every day they work. Many bullfighters are forced to retire at a young age because of injuries.

Bullfighter Will O'Connell tempts fate at the Hamel Rodeo in Corcoran, Minnesota.

Although the job is hazardous and the pay can be low, most rodeo clowns love what they do. They lead a thrilling lifestyle in which they can save lives and make people happy.

Bullfighter Patrick Crawford earns his pay at the Hamel Rodeo in Corcoran, Minnesota.

GLOSSARY

BRAHMA (OR BRAHMAN)
A breed of cattle that originated in India. Brahma bulls have a distinctive hump on the top of their shoulders. They are sturdy and able to withstand heat. They are often crossbred with other types of cattle, such as Hereford or Angus.

BULL ROPE
A flat, braided rope that is wrapped around a bull's chest. While sitting astride the bull, the cowboy adjusts his gloved hand around the bull rope. During the ride, he may not touch the bull rope with his free hand or he is disqualified. At the bottom of the rope is a bell. Its weight helps the rope fall off at the end of the ride.

CHUTE
A narrow pen where horses and bulls are held. Riders sit on animals in the chute. When the riders signal they are ready, the pen door is opened, and the animal charges into the arena.

FACE PAINT
Colorful paint used to create a pattern on a clown's face. It's an unwritten rule that each clown must create his or her own unique face design.

KEVLAR
A strong, lightweight man-made fiber used to make helmets, vests, and other protective gear.

PROFESSIONAL BULL RIDERS (PBR)
An international bull riding organization based in Pueblo, Colorado. It was begun in 1992 by a group of cowboys who wanted to promote bull riding.

PROFESSIONAL RODEO COWBOYS ASSOCIATION (PRCA)
The largest and oldest rodeo sanctioning organization in the world. It ensures that rodeos meet high standards in working conditions and livestock welfare. Located in Colorado Springs, Colorado, it sanctions about 600 rodeos in the U.S. and Canada.

RODEO
A Spanish word used by early cowboys when they gathered up their cattle. The English translation is "roundup."

INDEX